M000038970

GALE
CENGAGE Learning

Literary Themes for Students: The American Dream

Project Editor
Anne Marie Hacht

Editorial
Ira Mark Milne

Rights Acquisition and Management
Robbie Mc Cord, Lista Person, Kelly Quin, Andrew Specht

Manufacturing
Rita Wimberley

Imaging
Lezlie Light and Robyn Young

Product Design
Pamela A. E. Galbreath and Jennifer Wahi

Vendor Administration
Civie Green

Product Manager
Meggin Condino

© 2007 Gale, a part of Cengage Learning Inc.

Cengage and Burst Logo are trademarks and Gale is a registered trademark used herein under license.

For more information, contact
Gale, an imprint of Cengage Learning
27500 Drake Rd.
Farmington Hills, MI 48331-3535
Or you can visit our Internet site at
http://www.gale.com

ALL RIGHTS RESERVED
No part of this work covered by the copyright hereon may be reproduced or used in any form or by any means—graphic, electronic, or mechanical, including photocopying, recording, taping, Web distribution, or information storage retrieval systems—without the written permission of the publisher.

For permission to use material from this product, submit your request via Web at http://www.gale-edit.com/permissions, or you may download our Permissions Request form and submit your request by fax or mail to:

Permissions Department
Gale, an imprint of Cengage Learning
27500 Drake Rd.
Farmington Hills, MI 48331-3535
Permissions Hotline:
248-699-8006 or 800-877-4253, ext. 8006

Fax: 248-699-8074 or 800-762-4058

Since this page cannot legibly accommodate all copyright notices, the acknowledgments constitute an extension of the copyright notice.

While every effort has been made to ensure the reliability of the information presented in this publication, Gale, an imprint of Cengage Learning does not guarantee the accuracy of the data contained herein. Gale, an imprint of Cengage Learning accepts no payment for listing; and inclusion in the publication of any organization, agency, institution, publication, service, or individual does not imply endorsement of the editors or publisher. Errors brought to the attention of the publisher and verified to the satisfaction of the publisher will be corrected in future editions.

LIBRARY OF CONGRESS CATALOGING-IN-PUBLICATION DATA

Literary themes for students: the American dream: examining diverse literature to understand and compare universal themes / Anne Marie Hacht, editor; foreword by Margaret Brantley.
p. cm.—(Literary themes for students)
Includes bibliographical references and index.
ISBN-13: 978-1-4144-0433-2 (set: alk. paper)
ISBN-10: 1-4144-0433-6 (set: alk. paper)
ISBN-13: 978-1-4144-0285-7 (vol. 1: alk. paper)

ISBN-10: 1-4144-0285-6 (vol. 1: alk. paper)
[etc.]
1. American literature—History and
criticism. 2. American literature—Themes,
motives. 3. National characteristics,
American in literature. I. Hacht, Anne
Marie.
PS169.N35L58 2007
810.9'358—dc22 2007005602

ISBN-13:
978-1-4144-0433-2 (set)
978-1-4144-0285-7 (vol. 1)
978-1-4144-0286-4 (vol. 2)

ISBN-10:
1-144-0433-6 (set)
1-4144-0285-6 (vol. 1)
1-4144-0286-4 (vol. 2)

This title is also available as an e-book.
ISBN-13: 978-1-4144-2931-1
ISBN-10: 1-4144-2931-2
Contact your Gale, an imprint of Cengage Learning
sales representative for ordering information.

Printed in the United States of America
10 9 8 7 6 5 4 3 2 1

O Pioneers!

WILLA CATHER

1913

Willa Cather's 1913 novel, *O Pioneers!*, breathes new life into the American dream narrative using the landscape of the wild Nebraska prairie and a heroic female pioneer to tell a unique American immigrant success story. The title is taken from Walt Whitman's "Pioneers! O Pioneers!", a poem that, like the book, celebrates the spirit of the American frontier. Unlike pioneer tales told from the male perspective—including Whitman's poem

—*O Pioneers!* focuses on the powerful connection women have with the land and how that connection affects the settler experience.

Inspired by her own childhood spent on the prairies of Nebraska, Cather began writing her first Nebraska stories after essayist, fiction writer, and acquaintance Sara Orne Jewett advised her in a letter in 1908 to "find your own quiet center of life and write from that." Until she was nine years old, Cather lived near the town of Winchester, Virginia, in the Shenandoah Valley. Her ancestors had cultivated the lush land since the late eighteenth century, so it was a shock when her family left their prosperous farm and moved to wind-swept Red Cloud, Nebraska. According to Amy Ahearn's biography of the writer, Cather "had trouble adjusting to her new life on the prairie: the all-encompassing land surrounded her, making her feel an 'erasure of personality.'" The shock eventually wore off, though, and the immigrant community and geography of the mid-Western plains became for Cather personal touchstones and professional signatures. Ahearn writes, "It was to this land and these people that her mind returned when she began writing novels."

O Pioneers! is Cather's second novel, and the first of her trilogy of Nebraska novels. After *O Pioneers!* came *The Song of the Lark* (1915) and *My Antonia* (1918). Of Cather's many novels, poems, short stories, and essays, the books of the Nebraska trilogy are her most well-loved and critically acclaimed. *O Pioneers!*, published when the author was forty years old, established Cather as a writer of national significance. According to Kathleen Norris's essay "Willa Cather," the year the book was published one critic wrote, "Here at last is an American novel, redolent of the Western prairies." In 1931, Louise Bogan says of Cather in a *New Yorker* article, the author "used her powers ... in practicing fiction as one of the fine arts" and praises her for not being among those "writers of fiction who compromised with their talents and their material in order to amuse or soothe an American business culture."

Cather's allegiance to the people and the land of late nineteenth-century Nebraska make *O Pioneers!* a remarkable book. Her lyrical descriptions of the Nebraska landscape and the detailed characterizations she gives the immigrants that populate her prairie fiction could only be written by someone who had, according to Bogan, "made friends with her neighbors" and "learned all there was to know about the prairie, including how to kill rattlesnakes and how prairie dogs built their towns." This fictionalized dedication and knowledge also provide a view into a world rarely seen in American dream narratives. By teaming a feminist perspective with a disregard for traditional literary ideals—very few writers of the time would dare write fiction about ordinary working people—Cather created a new kind of American literature that continues to resonate with readers and critics to this day.

Part 1: The Wild Land

Chapter 1

The first chapter of the novel opens on a cold, windy day in the small town of Hanover, Nebraska, in the late nineteenth century. "Low drab buildings" are "huddled on the gray prairie, under a gray sky." Very few people inhabit the simple main street, except for a few "rough-looking countrymen in coarse overcoats" and a little Swedish boy who sits crying on the sidewalk. His clothes are worn and ill-fitting and he goes unnoticed by passersby. He is distraught because his kitten has been chased up a pole and is now too frightened to come down.

BIOGRAPHY
WILLA CATHER

Willa Sibert Cather was born in Back Creek Alley, Virginia, on December 7, 1873. In 1883, the Cathers left their lush Shenandoah Valley farm and moved to Catherton,

Nebraska. A year later, they moved to Red Cloud, Nebraska, where young Willa tried to acclimate to the near-treeless prairie. Cather's independent spirit led her to take a "man's job" delivering mail on horseback; she also frequently dressed in men's clothing, wore her hair short, and, on occasion, went by the name "William." In 1895, Cather graduated from the University of Nebraska-Lincoln where she was a theater critic and columnist for the *Nebraska State Journal*. From 1906 to 1911, Cather worked as managing editor for *McClure's Magazine*. Encouraged by writer Sarah Orne Jewett, Cather left the magazine to pursue a career in fiction writing. Her first novel, *Alexander's Bridge*, was published in 1912, followed a year later by *O Pioneers!* (1913). The writer went on to become nationally recognized, winning a Pulitzer Prize for fiction in 1923 for her novel, *One of Ours*, and several other literary awards and honorary degrees to colleges, including the University of Nebraska, Yale University, and Columbia University. Cather died of a cerebral hemorrhage in New York City on April 24, 1947.

The little boy is relieved to see his sister, "a tall, strong girl," walking "rapidly and resolutely" toward him. The girl chides her brother, Emil, for bringing the kitten into town. Her attempts at trying to lure the kitten down prove unsuccessful, so she goes looking for her friend, Carl Linstrum, believing he might be of help. She finds him in the drug store, and he agrees to climb the pole with the aid of a pair of spikes and rescue the kitten. After retrieving the creature, Carl asks whether Alexandra, Emil's sister, has seen the doctor. She has come into town for the sake of her sick father, whom the doctor has agreed to see the following day. "But he says father can't get better; can't get well," Alexandra explains. Carl is sympathetic and goes to tend to his friend's team of horses in preparation for her and Emil's return home.

Alexandra goes to the general store to fetch her brother and finds him "playing with a little Bohemian girl, Marie Tovesky, who was tying her handkerchief over the kitten's head for a bonnet." The little girl is very pretty and delights everyone in the store with her city clothes and eyes that resemble "that Colorado mineral called tiger-eye."

As Alexandra prepares for the long ride home, she tells her friend, "I don't know what is to become of us, Carl, if father has to die. I don't dare think about it. I wish we could all go with him and let the grass grow back over everything." Carl, sympathetic though quiet, places a lantern at Alexandra's feet to help light her way home.

Chapter 2

The second chapter of part 1 begins with a description of the Divide, the plateau situated between the Little Blue and Republican Rivers, where the Bergson family lives. "On one of the ridges of that wintry waste stood the low log house in which John Bergson was dying." After eleven years, the man "had made but little impression upon the wild land he had come to tame," an idea he ponders while looking through his bedside window at his fields, stables, corral, and the grass beyond them. As he lies dying, forty-six-year-old Bergson thinks about his 640 acres and how he acquired and paid for them. Before she was twelve, he learned to trust Alexandra's "resourcefulness and good judgment" and appreciate her "strength of will." Her brothers, Lou and Oscar, were "industrious, but he could never teach them to use their heads about their work." When Alexandra returns from town, he calls her to him and explains that she is to lead the family after his death. She promises to never lose the land and calls Lou and Oscar to their father's room. Bergson tells his sons, "I want you to keep the land together and to be guided by your sister.... I want no quarrels among my children, and so long as there is one house, there must be one head."

Chapter 3

It is six months after John Bergson's death. Oscar, Lou, Alexandra, and their youngest brother, Emil, stop by Carl Linstrum's home and ask if he would like to join them: "We're going to Crazy Ivar's to buy a hammock." They find Ivar sitting in the doorway of his clay bank dwelling reading the Norwegian Bible. Emil and Alexandra join Ivar in his cave house while Lou, Oscar, and Carl inspect the pond. Once she has selected a hammock, Alexandra asks Ivar's advice about her hogs. He tells her that "the hogs of this country are put upon" and that she needs to "give them only grain and clean feed" and provide them with a sheltered sorghum patch. When Oscar and Lou overhear this, Lou says, "He'll fill her full of notions. She'll be for having the pigs sleep with us, next." That evening, Alexandra looks "to the sorghum patch, where she was planning to make her new pig corral."

Chapter 4

The Bergson family had prospered the first three years, but now hard times have "brought every one on the Divide to the brink of despair." Indebted farmers have to give up their land and foreclosures demoralize the county. Carl tells Alexandra that his family is selling their place, auctioning their stock, and moving back to St. Louis:

> You've stood by us through so much and helped father out so many times, and now it seems as if we were running off and leaving you to face the worst of it. But it isn't as if we could really ever be of any help to you. We are only one more drag, one more thing you look out for and feel responsible for.

Alexandra understands that the Linstrums must leave, but she is saddened to lose her only friend. She says, "I can't help feeling scared when I think how I will miss you—more than you will ever know.... We've never either of us had any other close friend." Carl promises to write and work for himself as much as for her. "I want to do something you'll like and be proud of. I'm a fool here, but I know I can do something!"

That night, Alexandra tells Oscar and Lou about the Linstrums' plan to leave. At this, Lou replies, "You see, Alexandra, everybody who can crawl out is going away. There's no use of us trying to stick it out, just to be stubborn. There's something in knowing when to quit." This sets off an argument between the siblings. The boys think they should trade their land for a place near the river. Alexandra argues that the people who are running off are bad farmers: "They couldn't get ahead even in good years, and they all got into debt while father was getting out." She reminds her brothers that her father was set on keeping their land, that the family had struggled through harder times than this. Mrs. Bergson, depressed by this talk, cries and says she will never move. After thinking a while, Alexandra decides to investigate the river farms and see if the settlers there are really doing any better than the Divide settlers.

Chapter 5

The final chapter of part 1 begins with a description of Alexandra and Emil's trip to the river farms. After driving up and down the valley for five days, Alexandra decides the family is better off where they are. She tells Emil on their way back home, "Down here they have a little certainty, but up with us there is a big chance ... I want to hold on harder than ever, and when you're a man you'll thank me."

The evening of their return, Alexandra holds a family meeting and reports what she found beyond the valley. She explains to the boys her plan to "raise every dollar we can, and buy every acre we can." This includes selling off their cattle and mortgaging the homestead, an idea that upsets Oscar and Lou, who do not share Alexandra's vision of the future. After giving her brothers some time to think, Oscar, as much as he dreads signing "his name to them pieces of paper," declares, "We're in so deep now, we might as well go deeper." He is scared of the uncertainty, but knows that Alexandra is only looking for an easier way for them to get ahead.

Part 2: Neighboring Fields

Chapter 1

The first chapter of part 2 finds the Divide "thickly populated" sixteen years after John Bergson's death. Mrs. Bergson now lies buried beside him, the fields above them now a "vast checker-board, marked off in squares of wheat and corn; light and dark, dark and light." Emil Bergson sharpens his scythe "at the gate of the Norwegian graveyard" where his parents lie. Home from college, Emil is now a tall and handsome twenty-one-year-old captain of the track team, interstate record-holder in the high jump, and university band cornet player. Marie Shabata, previously Marie Tovesky, stops by to offer Emil a ride home.

A description of Alexandra's house finishes the

chapter. "There were so many sheds and outbuildings grouped about it that the place looked not unlike a tiny village." Her big white house on a hill was marked by a "most unusual trimness and care for detail." The three young Swedish girls Alexandra keeps to cook and clean enjoy a pleasant kitchen, and guests are surrounded by "the old homely furniture that the Bergsons used in their first log house," family portraits, and a "few things her mother brought from Sweden" in the sitting room.

Chapter 2

Emil finds Alexandra being waited on by her three young Swedish housegirls while lunching with "her men." In attendance is Ivar, a member of Alexandra's household ever since he "lost his land through mismanagement a dozen years ago." Though fuller, Alexandra is much the same. She discusses farm business with her men, especially the silo she had put up months before. One of the men mentions that Alexandra's brother Lou had said "he wouldn't have no silo on his place if you'd give it to him." Alexandra replies, "Lou and I have different notions about feeding stock, and that's a good thing. It's bad if all the members of a family think alike. They never get anywhere." Alexandra, after noticing Ivar's silence over lunch, asks him into the sitting room so that they might talk. He expresses his fear of being sent away to an asylum because he has been "touched by God." He wails, "They say that you cannot prevent it if the folk complain of me, if your brothers complain to the authorities. They say that your brothers are afraid—God forbid!

—that I may do you some injury when my spells are on me." Alexandra consoles the old man, saying,

> Ivar, I wonder at you, that you should come bothering me with such nonsense. I am still running my own house, and other people have nothing to do with either you or me. So long as I am suited with you, there is nothing to be said.

Chapter 3

Alexandra's family comes to dinner. The dining room is set for company, with "colored glass and useless pieces of china" because "her guests liked to see about them these reassuring emblems of prosperity." The party includes Alexandra, Lou, his wife Annie, their three daughters, and Oscar and his four sons. Lou tells Alexandra that he spoke to the superintendent of the asylum about Ivar's symptoms. "He says he's likely to set fire to the bar any night, or to take after you and the girls with an axe." When he tells Alexandra that it is just a matter of time before the neighbors have Ivar "taken up by force" she responds, "I'll have myself appointed Ivar's guardian and take the case to court, that's all. I am perfectly satisfied with him."

Carl Linstrum arrives in a buggy and he and Alexandra share an excited reunion. He asks if he might stay a few days as he is on his way to the coast. He explains that he is a fortune hunter on his way to the goldfields of Alaska and expresses wonder at Alexandra's place. "I would have never believed it could be done. I'm disappointed in my own eye, in my imagination." Oscar and Lou seem apprehensive in Carl's company and press their old neighbor about his business up north. Out of Carl's earshot, Lou asks Alexandra, "What do you suppose he's come for?" He does not think Carl has made much of himself and sees his traveling as "wandering." Oscar says, "He never was much account."

Chapter 4

Carl asks Alexandra how she and her neighbors became so successful. Alexandra replies, "We hadn't any of us much to do with it, Carl. The land did it. It had its little joke. It pretended to be poor because nobody knew how to work it right; and then, all at once, it worked itself." The two old friends talk about how they miss the old, wild country and the people who are gone. Alexandra tells Carl about Marie Tovesky, how she married Frank Shabata and moved into the Linstrum's old place. "Your farm took her fancy, and I was glad to have her so near me. I've never been sorry, either."

Chapter 5

Carl wakes early and walks to where "the Bergson pasture joined the one that had belonged to his father." This was where he and Alexandra used to "do their milking together, he on his side of the fence, she on hers." After a while, he comes upon Emil and Marie duck hunting. Carl does not make his presence known and he watches as Marie is initially thrilled by Emil's successful shot, then tearful when she collects the dead bird. Even though she was the one that invited Emil hunting, she is distressed by the act itself. "I hate to see them when they are first shot. They were having such a good time, and we've spoiled it all for them." Emil tries not to be cross with her, and Carl notices that, "as he looked down into her tearful eyes, there was a curious, sharp young bitterness in his own."

Chapter 6

Alexandra and Carl visit Marie. The three sit under a white mulberry tree and talk, giving Carl a chance to watch the two women together. As they leave, Carl and Alexandra run into Frank Shabata. He barely acknowledges them and begins yelling at his wife about the hogs he found in his wheat. The guests take their leave, and Marie is left to soothe her furious husband. "She was perfectly aware that the neighbors had a good deal to put up with, and that they bore with Frank for her sake."

Chapter 7

This chapter describes how Marie and Frank Shabata came to be married. Frank, as a young man, is described as a fancy-dressing, cane-carrying dandy with an eye for Marie Tovesky. When Marie told her father she was to marry Frank, "Albert Tovesky took his daughter, pale and tearful, down the river to the convent." After Marie turned eighteen, she ran away with Frank. Her father forgave her and bought she and Frank the Linstrum farm. "Since then her story had been a part of the history of the Divide."

Chapter 8

Marie sees Emil mowing on her way to pick cherries. Their conversation turns to Carl Linstrum and Marie says she has always wondered if Alexandra was a little in love with him. Emil is shocked and says, "Alexandra's never been in love, you crazy! She wouldn't know how to go about it. The idea!" He mentions that he would like to talk "to Carl about New York and what a fellow can do there." This sets off an argument between them that ends with Marie saying, "Then all our good times are over." Emil replies, "Yes; over. I never expect to have any more."

Chapter 9

It is a month after Carl Linstrum's arrival. He and Emil travel to the French country to attend a Catholic fair. Amédée, Emil's best friend, teases Emil for not having a girl. He loves being married and wants his friend to know the same joy. "Are you stuck up, Emil, or is anything the matter with you? I never did know a boy twenty-two years old before that didn't have no girl." Emil thinks it "strange that now he should have to hide the thing that Amédée was so proud of, that the feeling which gave one of them such happiness should bring the other such despair."

Chapter 10

Lou and Oscar pay Alexandra a visit. They have come to find out when Carl will be leaving. They announce that people in town have begun to talk and accuse her of making their family look ridiculous. When Alexandra suggests she may, in fact, want to marry her old friend, Lou says, "Can't you see he's just a tramp and he's after your money?" This sets off an argument over Alexandra's property—the real source of the boys' concern. They feel her land belongs to the family, but she tells them that if she wants to marry Carl and leave her property to him, she will. Alexandra tells them, "I think I would rather not have lived to find out what I have to-day."

Chapter 11

Emil tells Alexandra that he wants to put off law school for another year. He plans "to go down to the City of Mexico to join one of the University fellows who's at the head of an electrical plant" and see about a job instead. Alexandra tells Emil about her fight with Lou and Oscar and how she might want to marry Carl. Emil tells his sister that she should do as she wishes, that he will always support her.

Chapter 12

Carl, pale and tired-looking, tells Alexandra that, after seeing Lou and Oscar, he has decided to go away. "What a hopeless position you are in, Alexandra! It is your fate to be always surrounded by little men." He counts himself among them because he is "too little to face the criticism of even such men as Lou and Oscar." Alexandra tries to talk Carl into staying, but he feels he needs to have something to show for himself to be worthy. She says, "All at once, in a single day, I lose everything; and I do not know why."

Part 3: Winter Memories

Chapter 1

In the first chapter of part 3, winter has settled over the Divide. Emil sends Alexandra weekly letters, but Lou and Oscar have stayed away since Carl took his leave. Old Mrs. Lee comes for her yearly stay with Alexandra. Marie invites the two women to visit when Frank goes into town for the day. Alexandra brings Marie a bunch of Emil's letters to read and Marie gives her a silk necktie to send in his "Christmas box." While looking for crochet patterns for Mrs. Lee, Marie and Alexandra find Frank's old cane. The women laugh over the foolishness of the cane, then Marie turns thoughtful and says, "He ought to have a different kind of wife.... I could pick out exactly the right sort of woman for Frank —now." Alexandra believes that speaking so frankly about such things is a bad idea, so she distracts Marie by bringing her attention to the patterns.

Chapter 2

An omniscient narrator describes Alexandra's one and only fancy. It persisted from girlhood to adulthood, and lately visited her when she was very tired. As a child, it came to her on Sunday mornings, as she lay in bed listening to familiar sounds:

> Sometimes, as she lay luxuriously idle, her eyes closed, she used to have an illusion of being lifted up bodily and carried lightly by some

one very strong. It was a man, certainly, who carried her, but he was like no man she knew; he was much larger and stronger and swifter, and he carried her as easily as if she were a sheaf of wheat.

Part 4: The White Mulberry Tree

Chapter 1

Alexandra escorts Emil, who returned the night before from Mexico, to the French church supper in Sainte-Agnes. As they ride along, Alexandra thinks that all her family's hard work has paid off:

> Both Emil and the country had become what she had hoped. Out of her father's children there was one who was fit to cope with the world, who had not been tied to the plow, and who had a personality apart from the soil.

During dinner, Marie only takes "her eyes from Emil to watch Frank's plate and keep it filled." After playing charades and participating in the auction, Marie retires to her booth and begins telling fortunes. After a while, Emil approaches her booth, gives her a handful of uncut turquoises, and kisses her when the lights go out. "The veil that had hung uncertainly between them for so long was dissolved."

Chapter 2

This chapter opens at the end of the wedding supper for Signa, one of Alexandra's housekeepers, and Nelse, one of Alexandra's "men." Marie hurries home from Alexandra's, followed by Emil. He asks her why she ran away with Frank Shabata and she answers that she was in love with him. Then he asks her to go away with him. "Emil! How wickedly you talk! I am not that kind of a girl, and you know it. But what am I going to do if you keep tormenting me like this?" Emil promises to leave her alone if she says she loves him. When she admits, in her own way, that she does, he leaves her standing at her gate.

Chapter 3

A week after the wedding, Emil is packing. Alexandra shares memories of their father, of whom Emil remembers little, and assures him that he would have been proud of their father. "Alexandra felt that he would like to know there was a man of his kin whom he could admire."

Chapter 4

The fourth chapter of part 4 opens in the kitchen of Angélique and Amédée's house. Emil arrives and Angélique tells that Amédée is out cutting wheat, even though he is very sick. Emil rides out to the wheat field where he finds Amédée sitting atop his new header. The farmer is in obvious pain, but he insists he must keep working. Unable to convince his friend to stop, Emil rides to Sainte-Agnes, where he bids some friends goodbye. On his way home, he sees Amédée staggering out of the wheat field, supported by his two cousins. Emil helps get Amédée into bed.

Chapter 5

Frank Shabata receives news that Amédée was to be operated on "as soon as the Hanover doctor got there to help." Before heading to Sainte-Agnes, he tells Marie the bad news. After Frank leaves, Marie calls Alexandra who was comforted by her friend's voice. The older woman tells Marie that she already knew about Amédée's appendicitis, and that Emil, who had stayed with Amédé until he was operated on, was sick himself and already in bed. In the morning, Alexandra has to tell Emil that Amédée died hours earlier.

Chapter 6

Half of the community is dressing in white and preparing for the great confirmation service, while the other is dressing in black in preparation of Amédée's funeral. At the church, Emil notices that Frank arrives without Marie, which makes him begin to worry about her. Before he knows it, he is headed to Marie's house, where he joins her lying beneath the mulberry tree.

Chapter 7

Frank Shabata arrives home, disagreeable and slightly drunk, to find Emil's mare in his stable. When he steps into the house and hears no sound, he becomes suspicious and fetches his "murderous 405 Winchester from the closet." At the corner of his wheat field, he hears a murmuring. He shoots at two shaded figures lying beneath the mulberry tree, only to discover that he has shot Emil and Marie.

Chapter 8

Ivar notices that there is something wrong with Emil's mare. Scuttling across the fields to reach the nearest neighbor, Ivar mumbles, "Something is wrong with that boy. Some misfortune has come upon us." Before long, he reaches the Shabata orchard and finds the lifeless bodies of Emil and Marie.

Part 5: Alexandra

Chapter 1

Part 5 opens place three months later. A storm has brought rain, dark clouds, and cold winds, and Signa cannot find Alexandra. Ivar takes a wagon to the graveyard thinking he might find her there. She meets him at the graveyard gate and apologizes for worrying him. On their way back home, Alexandra tells Ivar, "I think it has done me good to get cold clear through like this, once. I don't believe I shall suffer so much any more." Once home, Alexandra feels that she is tired of life and longs to be free from her body. Before falling asleep, she experiences, again, the sensation of being lifted and carried by someone very strong.

When she wakes up, she decides to visit Frank Shabata. She blames herself for "throwing Marie and Emil together" and not seeing how they might have had feelings for one another. Her feelings for

Carl begin to wane after not hearing anything from him in weeks. She begins to wonder if she might "do better to finish her life alone."

Chapter 2

Alexandra travels to Lincoln. When she visits Frank in jail, she tells him, "I understand how you did it. I don't feel hard toward you. They were more to blame than you." Frank cries and explains how he never meant to hurt either of them. Alexandra sees that the man's personality has completely changed; he seems to her not altogether human. After they talk for a while, Alexandra promises that she will never stop trying to get him pardoned. "I'll never give the Governor any peace. I know I can get you out of this place." When she arrives back at the hotel, she receives a telegram from Carl. He writes that he arrived in Hanover the night before and will wait for her.

Chapter 3

Carl and Alexandra are spending the afternoon in the sunny fields surrounding her home. Carl never received the letter Alexandra sent that told of Emil's death. As soon as he learned about it from a month-old San Francisco newspaper, he traveled night and day to reach her. He explains that he has to return to Alaska in the spring, but he plans on staying with Alexandra through the winter. She is relieved because, as she tells Carl, he is all she has in the world. She says she would like to travel with him in the spring, but that she cannot go away for good. Carl understands and says, "You belong to the land,

as you have always said. Now more than ever."
They talk about getting married, and Carl kisses her
for the first time.

THEMES

Pioneer Spirit

Walt Whitman writes in his poem "Pioneers! O Pioneers!":

> All the past we leave behind;
> We debouch upon a newer, mightier world, varied world,
> Fresh and strong the world we seize, world of labor and the march, Pioneers! O pioneers!
> …
> We detachments steady throwing, Down the edges, through the passes, up the mountains steep,
> Conquering, holding, daring, venturing, as we go, the unknown ways, Pioneers! O pioneers!

His rugged, celebratory hymn to the pioneer spirit encompasses all that Cather sought to capture in her own ode to the independent, forward-thinking immigrants who tamed the Nebraska plains, especially in the post-Civil War years. America was still trying to define itself, and the influx of immigrants attempting to cultivate the western plains contributed to the country's transformation. After years of labor and thrift, many of these hard-working dreamers reached their goal of wealth and success: they made the American dream come true.

Romanticized in Whitman's poem, the challenging land of the prairies is so described by Cather in *O Pioneers!*: But the great fact was the land itself, which seemed to overwhelm the little beginnings of human society that struggled in its somber wastes. It was from facing this vast hardness that the boy's mouth had become so bitter; because he felt that men were too weak to make any mark here, that the land wanted to be let alone, to preserve its own fierce strength, its peculiar, savage kind of beauty, its uninterrupted mournfulness.

Anyone who ventured "the unknown ways" and attempted to interrupt the "mournfulness" of the land had to be prepared to fail. Many had no place else to go, and so died as they tried to carve out a life on the unforgiving plains. But while they fought to survive, they exemplified the pioneer spirit by looking forward, digging in, and making the most of what they had. In *O Pioneers!*, Cather writes, Alexandra often said that if her mother were cast upon a desert island, she would thank God for her deliverance, make a garden, and find something to preserve.... She had never quite forgiven John Bergson for bringing her to the end of the earth; but, now that she was there, she wanted to be let alone to reconstruct her old life in so far as that was possible.

The settlers' desire to reconstruct the lives they had known in France, Bohemia, Sweden, and Norway is echoed throughout the novel and is seen in the food they eat, the clothes they wear, the songs they sing, and the rituals they partake in. Over time, the varied cultures become a part of the American soil that is finally, after much struggle and strife, cultivated, fertile, and abundant with life and promise.

Women's Roles

In *O Pioneers!* Willa Cather creates an iconic American pioneer character that, until 1913, had yet to be imagined. In "Carving an Identity and Forging the Frontier: The Self-Reliant Female Hero in Willa Cather's *O Pioneers!*", Rula Quawas writes,

> Alexandra Bergson is a female hero who shifts the reader's perceptions of heroism, greatness, and nobility. She is a woman who embodies all the attributes admired in the finest of male characters in the American literary canon when faced with trials only a woman could confront. As a hero of the West, Alexandra breaks the concept of the untamed West and the woman's role in it.

Readers learn early on that John Bergson began consulting his daughter about farm issues before she was a teen:

> It was Alexandra who read the papers and followed the markets, and who learned by the mistakes of their neighbors. It was Alexandra who could always tell about what it had cost to fatten each steer, and who could guess the weight of a hog

before it went on the scales closer than John Bergson himself. Lou and Oscar were industrious, but he could never teach them to use their heads about their work.

The success of the family, their ability to progress both financially and personally, depended on the success of the farm, and the success of the farm, after her father's death, depended on Alexandra. John Bergson kept the American dream of working hard, saving, and becoming wealthy alive and passed it along to Alexandra because he believed that she, too, understood what it took to hold onto their land, against all odds, and make it grow. Father and daughter may have had different ways of weighing the value of the land—he saw it as the family's future, and she loved it as she loved herself—but both cherished it equally. In a telling passage at the beginning of *O Pioneers!*, Alexandra experiences a connection with the land that gives her faith in its future: For the first time, perhaps, since that land emerged from the waters of geologic ages, a human face was set toward it with love and yearning. It seemed beautiful to her, rich and strong and glorious. Her eyes drank in the breadth of it, until her tears blinded her. The the Genius of the Divide, the great, free spirit which breathes across it, must have bent lower than it ever bent to a human will before. The history of every country begins in the heart of a man or a woman.

In "Harvesting Willa Cather's Literary Fields," Beth Rundstrum writes, "Cather portrays harmonious relationships between women and land." She credits social, natural, and economic factors for these harmonious relationships, but lyrical descriptions of the land belie the fact that the author, herself an independent spirit with knowledge of Nebraska's cruel beauty, senses something in the connection that supercedes any single determining factor.

Homesteading

On May 20, 1862, President Abraham Lincoln signed into law the Homestead Act, a crucial piece of legislation in carving the American landscape and identity. By signing the act, Lincoln encouraged westward migration by offering parcels of 160 acres of public land to any household head over the age of twenty-one. Prospective homesteaders had to be willing to pay a small filing fee and five continuous years of residency on said land before receiving ownership of it. Immigrants, single women, former slaves, and farmers from the East with no land of their own all came forward with the requisite $18— the only money required—and a lot of hope. The parameters of the Homestead Act included a clause that stated that after six months of continuous residency, homesteaders had the option of purchasing land from the government for $1.25 per acre. This made it possible for homesteaders to add acreage to their own parcels over time, which, of course, made the offer that much more attractive. Because of the Homestead Act, eighty million acres of public land was distributed by 1900.

Most pioneers became homesteaders dreaming of a prosperous life on the Western Plains. Some settlers headed to Kansas, Nebraska, Colorado, and Wyoming with their families. Some went alone.

They knew farming uncultivated land would be tough, that living in a strange land far from other people would have its drawbacks, but the prospect of owning a piece of the American landscape—their own land—convinced them that the risk was worth it. But many were not prepared for the harsh reality of the homesteader's life. The isolation, with little or no social contact normally provided by schools, churches, or general proximity, was harder to bear than most settlers anticipated. Homesteaders also experienced the heartbreak of watching helplessly as swarms of grasshoppers devoured entire corn crops. Some lands were located in areas where rainfall was insufficient for successful farming. The soil in other regions was poor and difficult to farm. On the positive side, most settlers thought the country beautiful and worked hard to improve it. They built comfortable homes, sometimes out of sod if timber was unavailable or poor in quality, and accumulated land. Railroad access improved between 1860 and 1880, which made it possible to bring cattle to the homesteaders' farms and ranches. The Homestead Act was repealed in 1976, but provisions for homesteading in Alaska remained in effect until 1986.

CRITICAL OVERVIEW

In her critical interview with Willa Cather published in the August 8, 1931, *New Yorker*, Louise Bogan writes, "Miss Cather was not a young writer, as such things go, when she wrote *O Pioneers!*. She was thirty-eight. But at that age she found herself so certainly that she never again has needed to fumble about." The writer's sure handling of the story of Alexandra Bergson and her life as a successful homesteader on Nebraska's challenging Divide afforded Cather both an instant and longstanding reputation as a great American novelist. In 1913, one critic writes, "Here at last is an American novel, redolent of the Western prairies." Comparatively, Rula Quawas writes in her 2005 essay, "Carving An Identity and Forging the Frontier: The Self-Reliant Female Hero in Willa Cather's *O Pioneers!*",

> Cather's novel ... bridges the gap between gender and heroism. In this regional novel, Cather, who shows that women could do something important besides giving themselves to men, captures the essence of the heroic pioneer, the noble American spirit taming the West, in a female character.

Since gender studies came into vogue, *O Pioneers!* has been one of many American novels—and Alexandra Bergson one of many American literary characters—studied for its unique female perspective on a traditionally male-dominated topic. Beyond its reputation as a canonical work of feminist literature, the novel is also widely read as a critique of the effects of nineteenth-century industrialization. Beth Rudstrum wrote in the April 1995 *Geographical Review* article, "Harvesting Willa Cather's Literary Fields,"

> It is ... useful to analyze Cather's literary imagery. In *O Pioneers* she uses a recurring association of house, home, and homestead in the prairie landscape that symbolizes women. This image reflects the social values and cultural contexts in the United States at the time the novel was written, the early 1900s, and is Cather's prognosis for change in these values and history.... It is not unlikely that she used houses and homes to symbolize women on the prairie landscape in order to explicate women's social milieu during the late nineteenth and early twentieth centuries.

MEDIA ADAPTATIONS

O Pioneers! was adapted as a Hallmark Hall of Farm Productions film in 1992. Jessica Lange and David Strathairn play Alexandra and Carl under Glenn Jordan's direction. The film is available through Hallmark Hall of Farm Productions on DVD and VHS.

O Pioneers! was released in an abridged version on audiocassette by Penguin/Highbridge in 1994. It is narrated by Dana Ivey.

Some take issue with Cather's veiled criticism of American industrialization. Kathleen Norris writes, "The doctrinaire socialist and Marxist critics of the 1930s came to see Cather's work (as well as that of Sherwood Anderson, Sinclair Lewis, and other writers depicting small-town America) as reactionary." Michelle Abata quotes Marxist critic Granville Hicks in his scathing 1933 review. "The

Case against Willa Cather," in which he disparages Cather's "retreat to the past," derides her work's "supine romanticism," and posits that her fear of technology caused her to "recoil from our industrial civilization." This critique prompted Abate to write in her October 2006 *Hollins Critic* article,

> First uttered more than seventy years ago, Granville Hicks's disparaging remarks about Willa Cather continue to shape—and even haunt—critical views about her. Indeed, his observation that she "retreated to the past" has become the basis by which she is often critically disparaged and even canonically dismissed to this day.

Despite the criticism, and regardless of the sort of critical lens you use to view *O Pioneers!*, the novel stands as a unique work of American literature that inspires as much attention today as its author did in her time.

SOURCES

Abate, Michelle, "Willa Cather and Material Culture: Real-World Writing, Writing the Real World," in the *Hollins Critic*, Vol. 43, No. 4, October 2006, p. 16.

Ahearn, Amy, "Willa Cather: A Brief Biographical Sketch," in the *Cather Archive*, www.cather.unl.edu/life/brief_bio.html (November 1, 2006).

Bogan, Louise, "Profiles: American Classic," in the *New Yorker*, August 8, 1931; reprinted at www.cather.unl.edu/writings/bohlke/interviews/193 (November 1, 2006).

Cather, Willa, *O Pioneers!*, Houghton Mifflin, 1913; reprint, Barnes and Noble Classics, 2003.

Norris, Kathleen, "Willa Cather," *PBS American Masters Series*, www.pbs.org/wnet/americanmasters/database/cather (November 1, 2006).

"Primary Documents in American History: The Homestead Act," *Library of Congress*, www.loc.gov/rr/program/bib/ourdocs/Homestead.htl (November 1, 2006).

Quawas, Rula, "Carving an Identity and Forging the Frontier: The Self-Reliant Female Hero in Willa Cather's *O Pioneers!*," in *Studia Anglica Posnaniensia: International Review of English Studies, Vol. 41*, Annual 2005, pp. 237-50.

Rundstrom, Beth, "Harvesting Willa Cather's Literary Fields," in the *Geographical Review*, Vol. 85, No. 2, April 1995, pp. 217-28.

"The Homestead Act: What Was the Homestead Act?" *Homestead National Monument of America*, www.nps.gov/archive/home/homestead_act.html (November 1, 2006).

Whitman, Walt, "Pioneers! O Pioneers!", in *Leaves of Grass*, 1900, bartleby.com/142/153.html (January 11, 2007).

CPSIA information can be obtained
at www.ICGtesting.com
Printed in the USA
LVOW07s0835260817
546480LV00034B/293/P